Mr. Finnegan and the Bears

Once when we were homeless

Mr. Finnegan and the Bears

Once When We Were Homeless

Supokni

© 2019 Native Daughter Publications

ISBN: 9781095301395

for my grandchildren and those to follow

"Yes, Grandpa John used to say that the depression of today is worse than the depression of his day," Supokni spoke as she rocked that fussing baby, patting him softly on his back. "I guess he's right because when I was growing up I always had a bed to sleep in and a table full of food."

"Who is Grandpa John?" she asked the sleeping baby. "Well, he was my great grandfather," she laughed to herself. "That's just a little before your time."

The grandmother and the baby rocked in silence for a while. The baby on her shoulder began to squirm and fuss a bit. "OK, I'll tell you a story about a time when your daddy didn't have his own bed to sleep in. We were so poor we didn't have a 'pot to pea in' as Grammie often said."

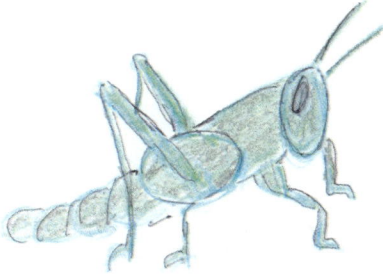

It was another grasshopper summer in the sun-washed apple mountains of middle New Mexico.

But for your daddy James it was the worst summer ever. That summer I was out of work, and we didn't have any place to live. We slept in a small dome tent in the mountains.

"I'll never forget because no one was willing to help us. It seems like when trouble comes, it separates us from all our friends. There was a time when our people helped each other. Now, we're all scattered like ragweed by the wind. No, my little one, it was a long way from the red desert of your daddy's people, the Diné."

At that time, it was just the four of us—me, your daddy, your Uncle Matthew, and Mr. Finnegan, of course.

Mr. Finnegan was definitely the best dog who ever lived. He really knew how to be a dog. James really loved that little dog. Most of the time, when I had to drive into town to look for work, your Uncle Matthew and your daddy stayed in the mountains.

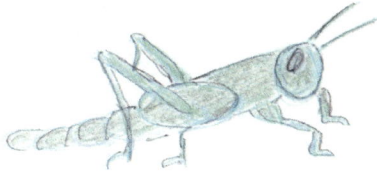

"*I think only Mr. Finnegan always wanted to play with your daddy. Your daddy was just a little boy then, you know. He was always precious to me because I lost the one before him.*"

Well, Mr. Finnegan and your daddy took long walks together through the cool forest.

They looked for frogs together in the little stream. They chased Deer. They laid in the cool fragrance of mint in a mountain meadow. James spent endless hours collecting and drying mint for tea.

"Yeah, your daddy was always a wonder that way. Life was full of discovery, and he insisted on sharing every little insight with his brother and me. It almost drove your Uncle Matthew nuts. You know he's the strong silent type."

The days were mostly lazy and fun. Your daddy really liked staying in the mountains. He could play all day and not have to take a bath at night. He could chew fresh mint until his tongue stung. Mostly he hated the nights. They were cold, dark, and a little scary. There were no other people for miles around and no bright streetlights to push back the darkness.

Every night we crawled into our sleeping bags inside that little bitty dome tent. We were so crowded that there wasn't even room to turn over. Mr. Finnegan always slept curled up on your daddy's pillow.

Worst of all, for your daddy, was that it was so dark that no one could read him a bedtime story.

"I never saw a child who loved to read like your daddy did. Lord, he sure did love it!"

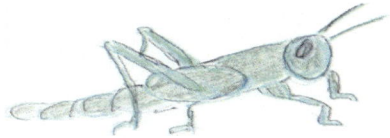

One night we had some excitement. A very loud thump woke us up. Outside our tent we heard something rustling crumpled paper and empty cans in the trash dumpster at our campsite. Mr. Finnegan stood stiff-legged at the tent door, growling low. Your daddy sat up in his sleeping bag, but he couldn't see a thing in the darkness.

"What was that?" he asked.

"Sh-h-h! Some kind of animal. Hush Finnegan!" I whispered back.

Further away, we heard more thumping.

"What kind of animal?" your daddy asked, sleepily.

"I don't know. Maybe a raccoon," I answered, trying not to think of any other possibilities. "Go back to sleep. It sounds like it's going away."

Mr. Finnegan and your daddy could not go back to sleep for a long time. Your daddy lay awake in his fear, listening to your Uncle Matthew snore. "Brother, doesn't anything ever wake him?" he wondered. All night Mr. Finnegan growled low in his sleep.

All of us took a walk the next morning to figure out what kind of animal had visited our camp. All up and down that dirt road dumpsters had been overturned. Garbage was spread everywhere.

Your daddy said, "Raccoons can't overturn dumpsters."

It was a warm, sunny Sunday, and we didn't think anything else about the events of the night before. All morning we played and read stories together. After lunch, Mr. Finnegan began barking. We all ran out of the tent to find a black bear rummaging the garbage. Uncle Matthew ran toward it.

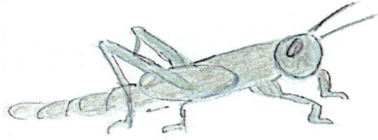

"You know, that boy never did have good sense. I used to tell him that he didn't have the sense that God gave a goose. If you've ever met a goose, you know about how much that is." Gently, Supokni lowered the baby to her lap, placing him gently on his stomach. One little arm spilled over the side.

Mr. Finnegan was a little dog, some kind of grey poodle-terrier mix. But he lit out after that bear like someone had set a fire under his tail. He was furious. Once that bear heard Mr. Finnegan, he turned tail and ran, just rocking like bears do when they run. Then your daddy and Uncle Matthew both ran after the two of them.

I hollered at them to "be careful," but they weren't listening. They were all caught up in the excitement and running like the wind. When they found that fool dog, he was dancing and barking at the foot of a pine tree. High up was a fat, baby bear. Mr. Finnegan had treed a bear.

Because Mr. Finnegan was our hero, he got his very own roasted hot dog that night. We all laughed and said what a good dog he was. His little button eyes, so full of life, shone back at us eagerly.

"Yeah, I reckon, I've never met a better dog ever. Everybody said so." Sʋpokni began to rub the baby's back.

After supper, your daddy and Mr. Finnegan took a stroll. The sun bent yearningly toward its night bunk, somewhere in the west. Its light made long monsters from the shadows of the trees.

James was watching his feet as usual, kicking up little puffs of dirt as he went along. Suddenly, one of the monster shadows rose up on its hind legs, pawing the air. It seemed to reach to the sky.

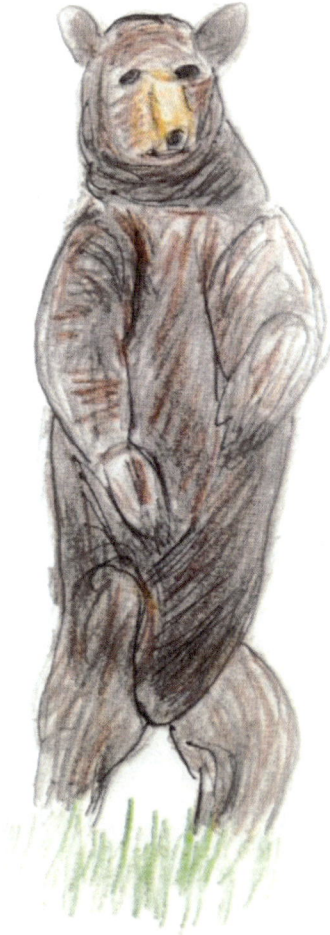

Your daddy froze, but not that fearless dog. In he charged, barking. For one long breath-stopping moment, the bear paused. Then she gently lowered herself to the ground and lumbered off into the gloom-gathering forest. Your daddy came thundering into our camp with Mr. Finnegan fast on his heels. He told all in one gushing rush.

"You see, my little one, that was a bad summer for bears, too. Poor, old things were so hungry that they were wandering all the way into the city and getting run over by cars. You know that in our way, Bear and People are related. Anyway, that summer we shared a lot with our cousin Bear. Too much, your daddy might say." Supokni laughed to herself as she brushed that soft baby hair.

That night, your daddy insisted that we all sleep in the van. But even in the van, your daddy never felt safe. That encounter with the bear had definitely taken the fun out of being homeless. It was only months later when I had another job and we had a house to sleep in that your daddy slept soundly. As for Mr. Finnegan, he always slept right next to the door just in case any stray bears tried to get in.

Sʋpokni laughed quietly as she lifted the now limp baby from her lap to put him in a crib. "Now, don't you go worrying about no bears. Sʋpokni's going to make sure you never have to live out of a van." Gently and firmly, she tucked in her sleeping grandbaby.

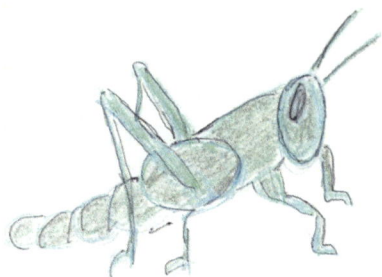

The End